A YEAR OF JOY

REFLECT AND WRITE WITH SONGS AND SCRIPTURE

INSPIRED BY THE GAITHER MUSIC LIBRARY
with Stephanie Castillo Samoy

ILLUSTRATED BY LAURA MARR

DOVER PUBLICATIONS
GARDEN CITY, NEW YORK

Introduction

Joy. It's such a little word for quite a big concept!

If you ask children what brings them joy, you may get these answers: candy, Santa Claus, toys, playing outside, Grandma and Grandpa, recess, cutting and pasting, riding a bicycle.

If you ask teenagers what they think of when you say, "joy," they may reply: getting the newest smartphone, receiving lots of likes on their latest social media post, scoring tickets to a sold-out concert, the high school football captain or homecoming queen acknowledging them, hanging out with friends, a brand-new outfit, keys to the car on Friday night, a letter of acceptance to their college of choice.

And for adults? What does joy conjure up? Vacationing with buddies. Getting reservations at a popular restaurant. Meeting the love of one's life. Being hired for one's dream job. Signing a lease on one's first apartment. The birth of one's child. Discovering a new skill set. Seeing the latest art exhibit.

Joy. What comes to mind when you think of this emotion, this expression, this state, this source? The word *joy* appears in the Bible somewhere between 150 and 430 times, depending on which version you have and what sources you refer to. Mother Teresa once said, "Joy is prayer; joy is strength; joy is love; joy is a net of love by which you can catch souls."

So here we are, drawn to *A Year of Joy*. Wanting to record in this journal all the joy that can happen in 365 days. Sometimes we need a little help uncovering these moments of happiness; finding felicity in the daily routines. We have partnered with Gaither Music Group, founded by Bill and Gloria Gaither, a GRAMMY Award–winning dynamic duo of gospel. They have graciously selected 52 of their favorite songs of joy, one for every week of the year, so that we may be inspired by the music while we journal.

From Gaither Vocal Band's "Because He Lives," "Amazing Grace," and "Low Down the Chariot," you'll find a range of tunes that will fill you with inspiration and delight. And alongside the Gaither performers, the artists who sing are a Who's Who of popular music: Alabama, Michael English, Mark Lowry, and Barbara Mandrell.

Scan the QR code below, choose your favorite streaming platform, and enjoy a playlist of 52 songs from the Gaither Music Library, lovingly curated for readers of this book. Inside, you'll find corresponding QR codes that lead to live recordings of the individual songs from the playlist. For a spiritual and multisensory experience, listen, watch, or sing along to the lyrics—some choruses are included on the printed page. In addition, a Scripture verse from the Bible complements each song. And we have offered a weekly "Touchstone" and prompts that may help you in your journaling.

Henri Nouwen (1932–1996), a priest and author, wrote: "Joy does not simply happen to us. We have to choose joy and keep choosing it every day."

Thank you for choosing *A Year of Joy*. May the songs fill your soul. May the Scripture verses make you whole. May the act of writing give you life.

GAITHER

Learn more about Gaither Music at Gaither.com

WEEK 1

Greatly Blessed, Highly Favored

Blessed be the God and Father of our
Lord Jesus Christ, who hath blessed
us with all spiritual blessings in
heavenly places in Christ.

—Ephesians 1:3

By Gaither Vocal Band from the album *Greatly Blessed*

Touchstone

As you begin *A Year of Joy*, think of a person, place, or thing that fills you with happiness. Stay with that for the week as you journal.

Like the song's title and lyrics, how are you greatly blessed and highly favored?

What are some of your imperfections? What steps can you take to correct them?

WEEK 2

I'm Gonna Sing

Chorus

I'm gonna sing just as long as it takes for a song
To make sad, heavy spirits free
I'm gonna keep making music that carries the secret
That Jesus is liberty
I'm gonna turn off the sounds that could drag people down
To the pit of despondency
With the sweet happy tune He is coming soon
For His children like you and me

By Gaither Vocal Band from the album *God Bless America*
Words by Gloria Gaither; Music by William J. Gaither and Woody Wright

Touchstone

Think about what weighs heavy on your heart.
Sing. Sing. Sing!

What is your favorite spiritual song?

Make a joyful noise unto the Lord, all the earth: make a loud noise, and rejoice, and sing praise.

—Psalm 98:4

How does it make you feel?

When do you find yourself singing?
When do you find yourself dancing?

WEEK 3

Amazing Grace

Amazing Grace, how sweet the sound
That saved a wretch like me (I once was lost)
I once was lost, but now I'm found
Was blind, but now I see

By Gaither Vocal Band from the album *Hymns*
Words and music by John Newton / Public Domain

TOUCHSTONE

This week, reflect on grace (God's and others') and what a gift it is in your life.

What does grace "sound" like to you?

And he said unto him, Son, thou art ever with me, and all that I have is thine. It was meet that we should make merry, and be glad: for this thy brother was dead, and is alive again; and was lost, and is found.

—LUKE 15:31-32

When in your life were you lost and blind?

Who found you?
How did you learn to see?

WEEK 4

I'm Gonna Live Forever

For God so loved the world,
that he gave his only begotten Son,
that whosoever believeth in him
should not perish, but have
everlasting life.

—John 3:16

By Ernie Haase & Signature Sound from the album
A Tribute to the Cathedral Quartet

Go outside this week to experience nature, and look for things that are eternal.

Do you want to live forever? What does that mean to you? Whom would you want with you in eternity?

Jesus was proclaimed "King of the Jews." How do you reconcile it with your faith identity?

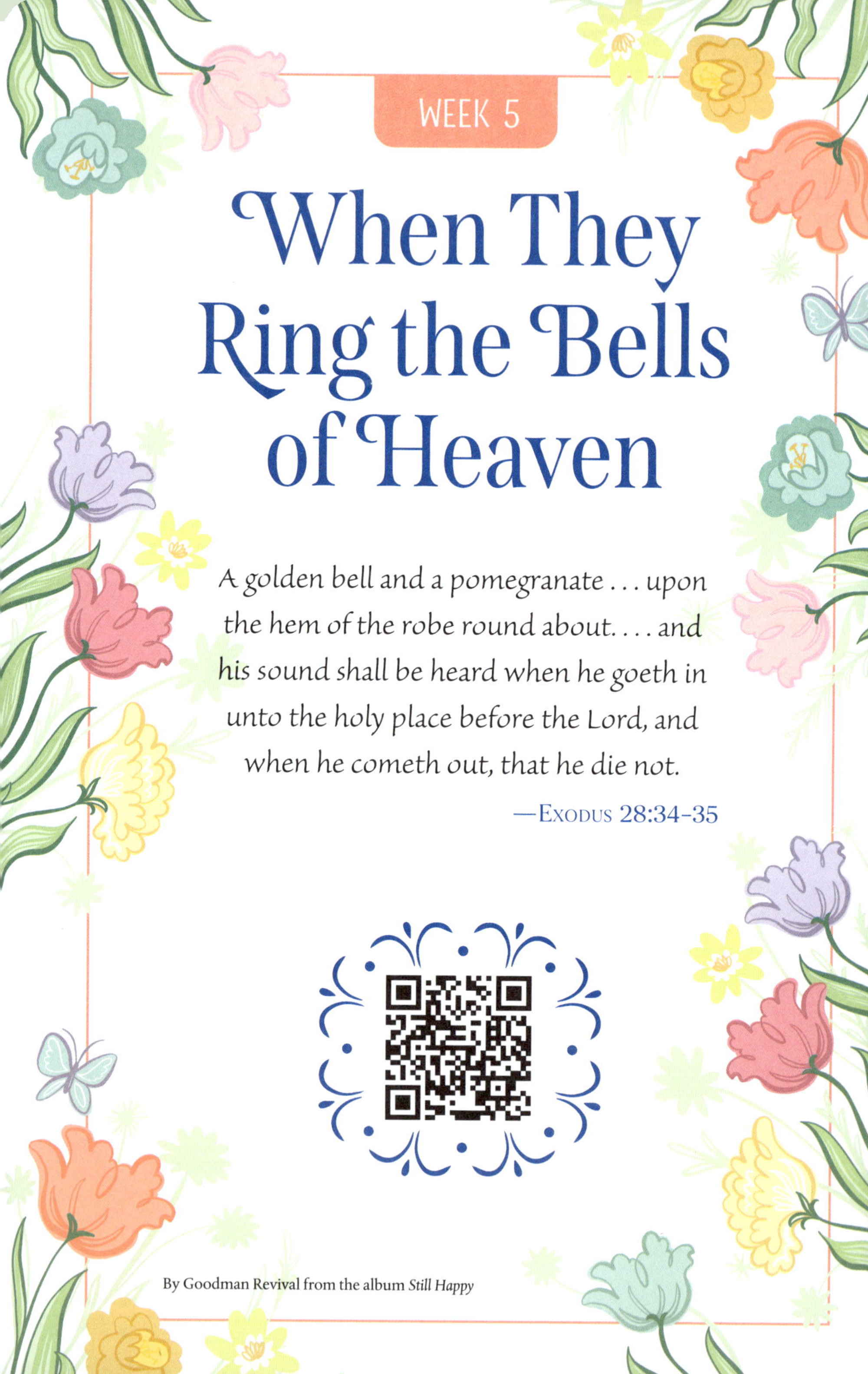

WEEK 5

When They Ring the Bells of Heaven

A golden bell and a pomegranate . . . upon the hem of the robe round about. . . . and his sound shall be heard when he goeth in unto the holy place before the Lord, and when he cometh out, that he die not.

—Exodus 28:34–35

By Goodman Revival from the album *Still Happy*

Touchstone

Keep your eyes and ears open to the sights and sounds of bells this week, and notice how they make you feel.

Sketch a bell and experience its form.

Where have you heard the ringing of bells? How would you characterize the sound?

WEEK 6

How Beautiful Heaven Must Be

Chorus

How beautiful heaven must be
Sweet home of the happy and free
Fair haven of rest for the weary
How beautiful heaven must be

By Gaither Vocal Band from the album *That's Gospel, Brother*
Words and Music by Mrs. A.S. Bridgewater
Additional Lyrics by Gloria Gaither

Touchstone

Reflect on the right here, right now and what you consider heavenly.

Do you believe in heaven?
How do you picture it?

And the twelve gates were twelve pearls; every several gate was of one pearl: and the street of the city was pure gold, as it were transparent glass.

—Revelation 21:21

What are the colors, scents, textures, shapes, flavors, and sounds of heaven?

How has your vision of heaven changed from when you were a child to now?

Pass Me Not, O Gentle Savior

Chorus

Savior, Savior
Hear my humble cry
While on others Thou art calling
Do not pass me by

By Gaither and Jason Crabb from the album *Sweet Hymns of Fellowship (Live)*
Words by Fanny J. Crosby; Music by William J. Doane

Touchstone

In the quiet of your day, reflect on those times when you lost belief in those who matter most to you.

Recall a time when you cried out to God.

My Lord, if now I have found favour in thy sight, pass not away, I pray thee, from thy servant.

—Genesis 18:3

Why was your spirit wounded and broken?

Where did the remorse come from?
What did your humble cry sound like?

WEEK 8

I'll Fly Away

The days of our
years are threescore years
and ten; and if by reason of
strength they be fourscore
years, yet is their strength
labour and sorrow; for it is
soon cut off, and we fly away.

—Psalm 90:10

By Bradley Walker, Ben Isaacs, and Mike Rogers from the album *Blessed: Hymns and Songs of Faith*

Imagine yourself flying and the feelings it evokes while listening to this week's song.

If you could fly, where would you go?
What happens to you when you die?

Do you believe in "a home on God's celestial shore"?

WEEK 9

Love Like I'm Leavin'

Then I commended mirth, because a man hath no better thing under the sun, than to eat, and to drink, and to be merry: for that shall abide with him of his labour the days of his life, which God giveth him under the sun.

—Ecclesiastes 8:15

By Gaither Vocal Band from the album *Good Things Take Time*

Touchstone

Each day this week, pretend it is your last day on Earth and think about how you would live differently.

How do you love?
Do you say what needs saying?

Do you pray what needs praying?
Do you laugh until it takes your breath away?

WEEK 10

Because He Lives

Chorus

Because He lives, I can face tomorrow
Because He lives, all fear is gone
Because I know He holds the future
And life is worth the living just because He lives

By Gaither Vocal Band from the album *Reunited*
Words by Gloria Gaither and William J. Gaither; Music by William J. Gaither

TOUCHSTONE

Reflect on eternal life and try to live in its promise before responding to the prompts this week.

Recall a time of uncertainty and how you dealt with it.

But this man, because he continueth ever, hath an unchangeable priesthood. Wherefore he is able also to save them to the uttermost that come unto God by him, seeing he ever liveth to make intercession for them.

—HEBREWS 7:24–25

What does it mean to you that "Jesus lives"?

How do you feel when you declare this to yourself?

Think about a moment when you had fear, and how you pushed through.

What makes your life worth living?

I Saw the Light

I am come a light into the world, that whosoever believeth on me should not abide in darkness.

—John 12:46

By Alabama from the album *Angels Among Us: Hymns & Gospel Favorites*

Touchstone

Look back on a moment in which you felt hopeless and reflect on how you chose to see the light.

When did you wander aimlessly?
How was your life filled with sin?

Who led you to the light?
Describe the moment you saw it.

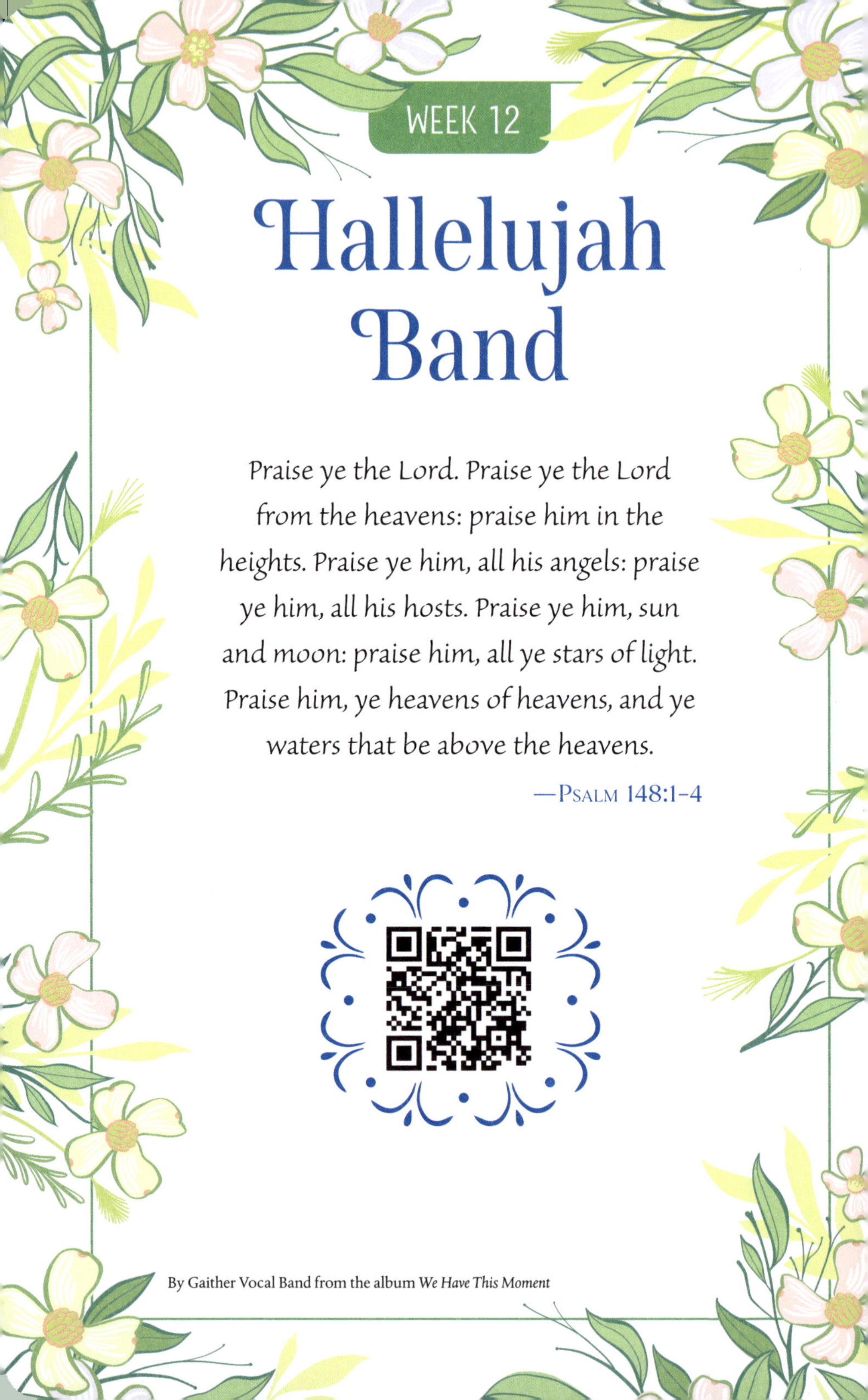

WEEK 12

Hallelujah Band

Praise ye the Lord. Praise ye the Lord from the heavens: praise him in the heights. Praise ye him, all his angels: praise ye him, all his hosts. Praise ye him, sun and moon: praise him, all ye stars of light. Praise him, ye heavens of heavens, and ye waters that be above the heavens.

—Psalm 148:1-4

By Gaither Vocal Band from the album *We Have This Moment*

Touchstone

At the end of each day this week, think of one "Hallelujah" moment.

Whom would you want in your Hallelujah Band? What kind of music would you perform?

Where would you tour? Who would be your audience? What instrument would you play?

WEEK 13

In the Garden

Chorus

And He walks with me, and He talks with me
And He tells me I am His own
And the joy we share as we tarry there
None other has ever known

By Barbara Mandrell from the album *Precious Memories: 20 Hymns and Gospel Classics*
Words and music by C. Austin Miles / Public Domain

Touchstone

Gardens are the perfect place to admire God's beauty. This week, take a moment to stop at one near you, look around, and delight in its resplendence.

Where do you walk with Jesus?

When Jesus had spoken these words, he went forth with his disciples over the brook Cedron, where was a garden, into the which he entered, and his disciples.

—John 18:1

Where do you best hear his voice?

What does he say to you?
What do you share with him?

WEEK 14

Great Is Thy Faithfulness (Lord Unto Me)

Chorus

Great is thy faithfulness, great is thy faithfulness
Morning by morning new mercies I see
All I have needed thy hand hath provided
Great is thy faithfulness, Lord unto me

By Jordan Smith from the album *The People's Hymnal*
Words by Thomas O. Chisholm; Music by William M. Runyan

Touchstone

Throughout this week, think about God's mercies and compassion and how they have made appearances in your days.

At times, do you feel your faith is slipping? Why? When do you feel your faith is strong?

It is of the Lord's mercies that we are not consumed, because his compassions fail not. They are new every morning: great is thy faithfulness.

—Lamentations 3:22–23

What does the lyric in this week's song, "All I have needed thy hand hath provided," mean to you?

What is your personal cross to bear?

He Lives

I am crucified with Christ:
nevertheless I live; yet not I,
but Christ liveth in me: and the
life which I now live in the flesh
I live by the faith of the
Son of God, who loved me,
and gave himself for me.

—Galatians 2:20

By David Phelps from the album *Hymnal*

Touchstone

Each day this week, live the way Christ lives and look for examples of his loving care around you before reflecting on the prompts.

Describe a time when Jesus walked with you and talked with you.

How do you experience his goodness and kindness? How do you serve Christ?

WEEK 16

Jesus Saves

Neither is there salvation in any
other: for there is none other
name under heaven given among
men, whereby we must be saved.

—Acts 4:12

By The Booth Brothers from the album *Gospel Favorites (Live)*

Touchstone

Set the example this week on what it means to you that "Jesus saves."

Do you need to be saved? What does that mean to you?

How do you find salvation? Where do you seek it? When have you experienced it?

I Believe in a Hill Called Mount Calvary

Chorus

I believe in a hill called Mount Calv'ry
I believe whatever the cost
And when time has surrendered
And earth is no more
I'll still cling to that old rugged cross

By Gaither Vocal Band from the album *Reunited*
Words by William J. and Gloria Gaither and Dale Oldham; Music by William J. Gaither

Touchstone

The road to Calvary represents Jesus's ultimate passion. Take a moment each day this week to think about your own road to Calvary.

What does it mean to "cling to the old rugged cross"?

And when they were come to the place, which is called Calvary, there they crucified him, and the malefactors, one on the right hand, and the other on the left. Then said Jesus, Father, forgive them.

—Luke 23:33-34

Imagine Mount Calvary in the time of Jesus.

Picture yourself in the scene as he is being hung on a cross. Where are you in that scene?

How do you glean hope and promise in this time of darkness and death?

How has Jesus changed your life?

WEEK 18

God Rides on Wings of Love

*How excellent is thy lovingkindness,
O God! therefore the children of men
put their trust under the
shadow of thy wings.*

—Psalm 36:7

By Janet Paschal from the album *Songs for a Lifetime*

This week, reflect on the lyrics
"I feel the winds of mercy."

When have you felt God's love?

What do "wings of love" look like to you?
Do you ever wear them? What is that like?

WEEK 19

There's Something About That Name

Chorus

Jesus, Jesus, Jesus; there's
just something about that name
Master, Savior, Jesus, like the fragrance after the rain
Jesus, Jesus, Jesus, let all Heaven and earth proclaim
Kings and kingdoms will all pass away
But there's something about that name

By Gaither Vocal Band from the album *Reunited*
Words by William J. and Gloria Gaither; Music by William J. Gaither

Touchstone

Take note of all the times throughout your day when you call out Jesus's name.

Where were you this week when you called out his name?

How did you feel?

What does the sound of Jesus's name arise in you?

Have you witnessed Jesus's strength in others?

Reflect on a moment when Jesus's name calmed you.

That at the name of Jesus every knee should bow, of things in heaven, and things in earth, and things under the earth.

—Philippians 2:10

WEEK 20

What a Wonderful World

In the beginning God created the heaven and the earth. . . . And God saw every thing that he had made, and, behold, it was very good. And the evening and the morning were the sixth day.

—Genesis 1:1,31

By David Phelps from the album *Classic*

Touchstone

In this classic song, beauty, relationships, and love are all around us. Take a break each day this week to stop and absorb your surroundings.

How does this song make you feel? What is in your "wonderful world"?

When is life wonderful? Who is wonderful? Where is wonderful?

WEEK 21

Going Home

Chorus

Going home I'm going home
There's nothing to hold me here
Well I've caught a glimpse
Of that heavenly land
Praise God I'm going home

By Josh Turner from the album *Award-Winning Artists Sing the Songs of Gaither*
Words by William J. and Gloria Gaither; Music by William J. Gaither

Touchstone

"Home" means different things to different people. This week, think about what "home" means to you.

What does home look like with Jesus?

Return to thine own house, and shew how great things God hath done unto thee.

—Luke 8:39

What does “going home” mean to you?

How does “going home” feel?

With whom would you want to share your home?

WEEK 22

Up Above My Head

And suddenly there was with the angel a multitude of the heavenly host praising God, and saying, Glory to God in the highest, and on earth peace, good will toward men.

—Luke 2:13–14

By Canton Junction from the album *Great Is Thy Faithfulness (Live)*

Touchstone

When you experience troublesome times this week, look up! Things will get better.

What is up above your head? Is it music? Is it heaven? Are there angels?

What do you believe?

That's Enough

Greater love hath no man than this, that a man lay down his life for his friends. Ye are my friends, if ye do whatsoever I command you.

—John 15:13–14

By Gaither and Babbie Mason from the album *Gospel Pioneer Reunion (Live)*

Touchstone

Each day this week, think about a friend and hold them with you in prayer.

Is Jesus enough for you?
When has he picked you up?

When has he stuck by you?
When has he taken care of your enemies?

WEEK 24

He Touched Me

Chorus

He touched me
Oh, He touched me
And oh, the joy that floods my soul
Something happened and now I know
He touched me
And made me whole

By Joey + Rory from the album *Hymns*
Words and Music by William J. Gaither

Touchstone

Make note of the way Jesus touches you in your day-to-day life and how you can be Jesus's heart and hands to those you encounter this week.

Think of a time when you were "shackled by a heavy burden."

And Jesus came and touched them, and said, Arise, and be not afraid.

—Matthew 17:7

How about when you were weighted by a load of guilt and shame?

Describe how Jesus touched you. What happened?

How were you made whole?

WEEK 25

That's Gospel, Brother

A new commandment I give unto you,
That ye love one another;
as I have loved you,
that ye also love one another.

—John 13:34

By Gaither Vocal Band from the album *That's Gospel, Brother*

Touchstone

You are almost at the halfway point in *A Year of Joy*. Think about your journey so far.

Whom do you walk with in this life?
Why are you bonded in this way?

What makes it "perfect harmony"?
What other gospel do you live by?

WEEK 26

The Seeker

With my whole heart have
I sought thee:
O let me not wander from
thy commandments.

—Psalm 119:10

By Lynda Randle from the album *By the Riverside*

Touchstone

Throughout this week, embody what it means to be "the seeker."

Would you call yourself a "seeker"?
What are you searching for?

Where do you look? How do you approach your pursuit?
Who accompanies you?

His Eye Is on the Sparrow

Chorus

So I sing because I'm happy
And I sing because I'm free
For His eye is on the sparrow
And I know He watches me

By Gaither and Larnelle Harris from the album *The Old Rugged Cross (Live)*
Words by Civilla D. Martin; Music by Charles H. Gabriel

Touchstone

This week, think about what it means to have God looking out just for you.

Describe the emotions that arise from this song and the Scripture verse.

Are not two sparrows sold for a farthing? and one of them shall not fall on the ground without your Father. But the very hairs of your head are all numbered. Fear ye not therefore, ye are of more value than many sparrows.

—Matthew 10:29–31

When have you felt discouraged?

What times has your heart been troubled?

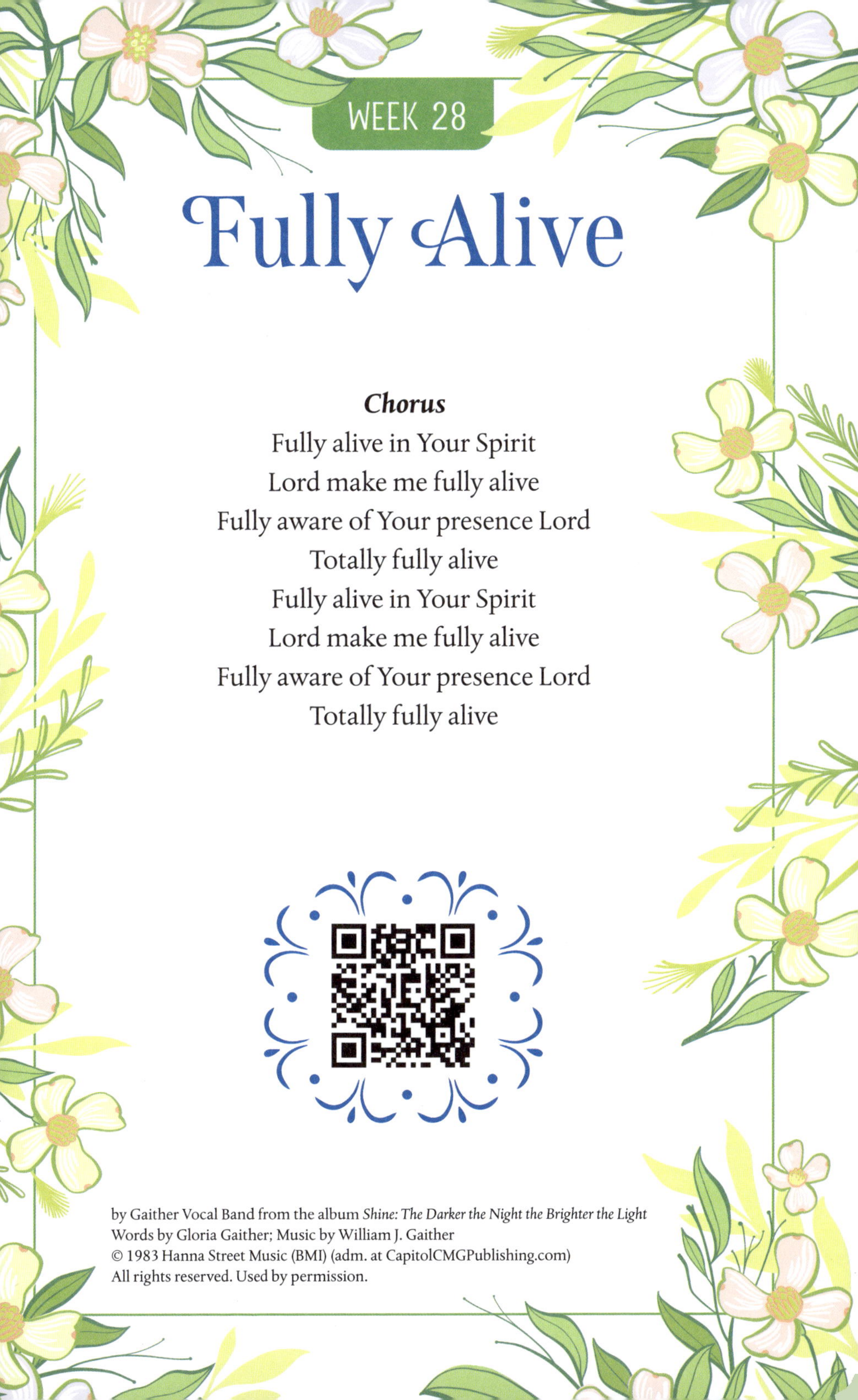

WEEK 28

Fully Alive

Chorus

Fully alive in Your Spirit
Lord make me fully alive
Fully aware of Your presence Lord
Totally fully alive
Fully alive in Your Spirit
Lord make me fully alive
Fully aware of Your presence Lord
Totally fully alive

by Gaither Vocal Band from the album *Shine: The Darker the Night the Brighter the Light*
Words by Gloria Gaither; Music by William J. Gaither

Touchstone

You don't have to do anything this week.
Just experience what it means to be fully alive.

How are you fully alive?

What glory surrounds you?

I am come that they might have life, and that they might have it more abundantly.

—John 10:10

Who are the ones you hold dear?

WEEK 29

You Can't Take My Joy

These things have I spoken unto you,
that my joy might remain in you,
and that your joy might be full.

—John 15:11

By The Isaacs from the album *Why Can't We*

Touchstone

When you find life getting a bit tough or challenging this week, remember the phrase "You Can't Take My Joy."

Where do you get your joy?
Is it in your home, money, reputation?

WEEK 30

Rivers of Joy

There is a river, the streams whereof shall make glad the city of God, the holy place of the tabernacles of the most High. God is in the midst of her; she shall not be moved: God shall help her, and that right early.

—Psalm 46:4-5

By Stephen Hill and Lillie Knauls from the album *Rivers of Joy*

Touchstone

Take note of the times this week when you are flooded by rivers of joy.

Is there an actual river that holds special meaning to you?

What is it about that body of water that brings you joy?

Roses Will Bloom Again

Chorus

Roses will bloom again, just wait and see
Don't mourn what might have been
Only God knows how and when
But roses will bloom again

By Jeff & Sheri Easter from the album *Sweeter as the Days Go By (Live)*
Words and Music by Marcia Henry

Touchstone

As you are in the second half of *A Year of Joy*, take it as an opportunity to begin again—a resurrection, if you will.

What is your favorite flower?

Jesus said unto her, I am the resurrection, and the life: he that believeth in me, though he were dead, yet shall he live: And whosoever liveth and believeth in me shall never die. Believest thou this?

—John 11:25-26

Knowing that it cannot last forever,
how does that make you feel?

Whom have you cherished and lost?
How did you find the will to go on?

WEEK 32

Swing Down Chariot

Chorus

Why don't you swing down (sweet) chariot
Stop and let me ride
Swing down chariot
Stop and let me ride
Rock me Lord, rock me Lord
Calm and easy
I've got a home on the other side

By Gaither Vocal Band and Ernie Haase & Signature Sound from the album *Together*
Words, Music and Arrangement by Gaither Vocal Band

TOUCHSTONE

This week, offer to help someone (friend or stranger). "Swing down your chariot!"

When have you needed a lift?
When have you offered one?

And it came to pass, as they still went on, and talked, that, behold, there appeared a chariot of fire, and horses of fire, and parted them both asunder; and Elijah went up by a whirlwind into heaven.

—2 KINGS 2:11

Think of a time when you experienced a figurative bumpy road in your life.

How about a time when that road was calm and easy?

We Are All God's Children

Beloved, now are we the sons of God, and it doth not yet appear what we shall be: but we know that, when he shall appear, we shall be like him; for we shall see him as he is.

—1 John 3:2

By Gaither Vocal Band from the album *We Have This Moment*

This week, think about your being a child of God and live that way.

Do you really believe that "we are all God's children"?

What does that actually mean?
How about those who hurt, maim, or kill?

WEEK 34

Victory in Jesus

Hereby perceive we the love of God,
because he laid down his life for us:
and we ought to lay down our lives
for the brethren.

—1 John 3:16

By Jimmy Fortune, Ben Isaacs, Gene McDonald, and Reggie Smith from the album *Hits & Hymns*

Touchstone

Live each day this week as if it were a "victory in Jesus."

How have you experienced "victory in Jesus"? Describe the journey to get there.

WEEK 35

I Just Feel Like Something Good Is About to Happen

Chorus

I just feel like something good is about to happen
I just feel like something good is on its way
God has promised that He'd open all of heaven
And, brother, it could happen any day

By Gaither Vocal Band from the album *That's Gospel, Brother*
Words and Music by William J. Gaither

Touchstone

When you find yourself feeling gloomy or overwhelmed this week, take a deep breath and know that this, too, shall pass.

Have you ever felt like something good is about to happen?

The wilderness and the solitary place shall be glad for them; and the desert shall rejoice, and blossom as the rose.

—Isaiah 35:1

And did it?

What did the anticipation feel like?

Were you grateful?

Did you thank God?

Wait'll You See My Brand New Home

In my Father's house are many mansions: if it were not so, I would have told you. I go to prepare a place for you. And if I go and prepare a place for you, I will come again, and receive you unto myself; that where I am, there ye may be also.

—John 14:2–3

By Chris Blue from the album *Foundations: The Hymns of My Heart*

Touchstone

When you find yourself at home this week, imagine the promise of eternity and your "brand new home."

How do you see your "brand new home"? What is it built from? Where is it located?

Who is there waiting for you? Who is welcome in it?

Joy Unspeakable

Chorus

It is joy unspeakable and full of glory
Full of glory, full of glory
It is joy unspeakable and full of glory
O the half has never yet been told

By Joy Gardner, Tanya Goodman Sykes, Wesley Pritchard, and Sarah DeLane
from the album *Homecoming Hymns*
Words and Music by Barney E. Warren

Touchstone

This week, keep a log of when you feel joy, gratitude, and hope before writing your responses.

Name a grace you received recently.

Whom having not seen, ye love; in whom, though now ye see him not, yet believing, ye rejoice with joy unspeakable and full of glory.

—1 Peter 1:8

Name a moment of happiness you experienced recently.

Name a pleasure you experienced recently.

Name a hope that materialized.

Name a joy that came your way.

WEEK 38

Count Your Blessings

Thou preparest a table before me
in the presence of mine enemies:
thou anointest my head with oil;
my cup runneth over.

—Psalm 23:5

By The Martins from the album *The Ultimate Playlist*

Touchstone

Blessings are abundant, even in difficult and trying times. Think about the many graces you have in your life this week.

Do you count your blessings? List three of them. Can you think of more?

Down by the Riverside

Chorus

Gonna lay down my burden
Down by the riverside
Down by the riverside
Down by the riverside
Gonna lay down my burden
Down by the riverside
I ain't gonna study war no more

By Lynda Randle from the album *Down by the Riverside*
Traditional African-American Spiritual

Touchstone

This week, spend some time at your "riverside," be it a quiet corner of a room, a favorite park bench, or an actual riverside.

What thoughts occurred while you were reflecting in nature?

And he shall judge
among the nations,
and shall rebuke many
people: and they shall
beat their swords into
plowshares, and their
spears into pruninghooks:
nation shall not lift up
sword against nation,
neither shall they learn
war any more.

—Isaiah 2:4

Where do you lay your burdens, your sword, and your shield?

What do you study when you are there?

What does your song of joy sound like?

What is it about your “riverside” that makes it your special place to be?

WEEK 40

Jesus Laughing

Then was our mouth filled with laughter, and our tongue with singing: then said they among the heathen, The Lord hath done great things for them.

—Psalm 126:2

By Mark Lowry and The Martins from the album *Dogs Go to Heaven (Live)*

Touchstone

"Laughter is the best medicine," goes the old adage.
This week, feel free and allow yourself
to have a hearty laugh.

Can you hear Jesus laughing? What is so funny?
What makes you giddy with the giggles?

Something Beautiful / Let's Just Praise the Lord

Chorus

Something beautiful, something good
All my confusion He understood
All I had to offer Him
Was brokenness and strife
But He made something beautiful of my life

By Gaither and Danny Gaither from the album *Something Beautiful (Live)*
Words by Gloria Gaither; Music by William J. Gaither

Touchstone

Notice something beautiful each day,
and take note of the sensations you feel.

Describe the beauty and goodness that you get from Jesus.
What do you offer in exchange for these gifts?

To appoint unto them that mourn in Zion, to give unto them beauty for ashes, the oil of joy for mourning, the garment of praise for the spirit of heaviness.

—Isaiah 61:3

List some examples of your confusion, brokenness, and strife.

How are they alleviated? What have you laid at the Cross?

WEEK 42

Give It Away

Chorus

If you want more happy than your heart will hold
If you wanta stand taller—if the truth were told
Just take whatever you have and give it away
If you want less lonely and a lot more fun
And deep satisfaction when the day is done
Then throw your heart wide open and give it away

By Gaither Vocal Band from the album *Special Anniversary Collection*
Words by Gloria Gaither; Music by Benjamin Gaither

Touchstone

St. Francis of Assisi prayed, "For it is in giving that we receive." This week, try to be more generous with your time, patience, and forgiveness to each person you encounter.

Are you a taker or a giver?
Are you a griper and complainer or a big-hearted liv-er?

Every man according as he purposeth in his heart, so let him give; not grudgingly, or of necessity: for God loveth a cheerful giver.

—2 Corinthians 9:7

How do you choose to spend your days?

Describe the state of your heart. How do you feel when you "give it away"?

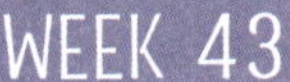

It's Shouting Time in Heaven

And I heard as it were the voice of a great multitude, and as the voice of many waters, and as the voice of mighty thunderings, saying, Alleluia: for the Lord God omnipotent reigneth. Let us be glad and rejoice, and give honour to him: for the marriage of the Lamb is come, and his wife hath made herself ready.

—Revelation 19:6–7

By The Hoppers from the album *The Best of The Hoppers*

Touchstone

When you feel like screaming out in anger this week, pause and imagine what shouting in heaven would sound like.

When were you lost and then found?
What sins of yours need forgiving?

What is being shouted in heaven about you?
Why is that message being declared?

WEEK 44

Joy Comes in the Morning

For his anger endureth but a moment; in his favour is life: weeping may endure for a night, but joy cometh in the morning.

—Psalm 30:5

By Gloria Gaynor from the album *Testimony*

Touchstone

This week, remind yourself of the power of joy, especially after those times of pain, loss, and stress.

When was your "darkest before the dawn"? Did the sun rise?

When did the storm hit? Was there calm afterward? Describe one of your joys in the morning.

The Center of My Joy

Chorus

Jesus, You're the center of my joy
All that's good and perfect comes from You
You're the source of my contentment,
hope in all I do
Jesus, You're the center of my joy

By Chris Blue from the album *Foundations: The Hymns of My Heart*
Words by Gloria Gaither; Music by William J. Gaither and Richard Smallwood

Touchstone

Think about all the things in your life that keep you centered.

Describe how Jesus is at the center of your joy.

Think of a time when you lost direction.

Remember a spell when the nights were long and cold.

And not only so, but we also joy in God through our Lord Jesus Christ, by whom we have now received the atonement.

—Romans 5:11

Recall a time when you were sad.

How did you get back to center?

WEEK 46

I'm Rich

Hearken, my beloved brethren, Hath not God chosen the poor of this world rich in faith, and heirs of the kingdom which he hath promised to them that love him?

—James 2:5

By Gaither Vocal Band from the album *Pure and Simple*

Touchstone

Being rich means more than just having material items. Take inventory of your figurative treasures, and express gratitude for them.

Are you rich?
What are your treasures?

What does it mean to be one of God's heirs?
What, if anything, will you inherit?

WEEK 47

Satisfied

Chorus

I'm satisfied (satisfied with Jesus),
I'm satisfied(satisfied with Jesus)
Said He would be my comfort,
said He would be my guide
Well, well, I looked at my hands,
my hands looked new
I looked at my feet, and they did too
Ever since that wonderful day,
my soul's been satisfied

By Michael English, Mark Lowry, Bill Gaither, and Wes Hampton from the album *Gaither Vocal Band—Reunion*
Words, Music and Arrangement by Gaither Vocal Band

Touchstone

This week take time to reflect and give gratitude for how satisfied you feel.

Describe your week's moment of gratitude. Where were you? What happened?

*For he satisfieth
the longing soul,
and filleth
the hungry soul
with goodness.*

—Psalm 107:9

Where did you meet Jesus?
Describe how you felt.

How would you characterize your relationship with him?

Is he your comfort and your guide? Write about an occasion when he comforted and guided you.

When do you feel satisfied?

WEEK 48

Sweeter as the Days Go By

O taste and see that the Lord is good:
blessed is the man that trusteth in him.

—Psalm 34:8

By The Collingsworth Family from the album *Classics & Hymns*

Think about what makes your life "sweeter as the days go by" this week.

What makes life sweet for you?

When has God's love made itself known?
Who shares all of this with you?

WEEK 49

Low Down the Chariot

Some trust in chariots, and
some in horses: but we will
remember the name of the
Lord our God.

—Psalm 20:7

By Gaither Vocal Band from the album *Better Day*

Touchstone

This week, "low down the chariot" and give someone a ride or accompany them to an appointment. In other words, help them out!

Whom did you help this week? Describe it.

If you had a chariot, where would you want to ride?

Would you be the sole occupant?
Would you be driving or riding along?

Who would your passengers be? Why them?

WEEK 50

Glory, Glory Clear the Road

Let us lay aside every weight, and the sin which doth so easily beset us, and let us run with patience the race that is set before us, looking unto Jesus the author and finisher of our faith.

—Hebrews 12:1–2

By Old Friends Quartet from the album *Encore: Old Friends Quartet*

Touchstone

Check in with yourself each day this week on the state of the path you are pursuing.

How is your running of the race going right now? Where are you on the course?

Who is cheering you along the sidelines? How are they encouraging you?

At the Cross

Chorus

At the cross, at the cross where I first saw the light
And the burden of my heart rolled away
It was there by faith I received my sight
And now I am happy all the day

By Gaither and Adam Crabb from the album *Sweet Hymns of Fellowship (Live)*
Words by Isaacs Waats; Music by Ralph E. Hudson; Arr. by Ronn Huff

Touchstone

Imagine yourself at the Cross and allow the graces to come forth.

What burdens are you carrying?

Who his own self bare our sins in his own body on the tree, that we, being dead to sins, should live unto righteousness: by whose stripes ye were healed

—1 Peter 2:24

When did you bring these to Jesus?
How did he respond?

Where are you now?

WEEK 52

Joy

The joy of the Lord is your strength.

—NEHEMIAH 8:10

By Mark Lowry from the album *There Is Hope*

Touchstone

As you reach the end of *A Year of Joy*,
reflect on all the moments that captured that
emotion and savor them with a grateful heart.

When were you broken, torn, or tattered?

When did your world crumble and no one was there?

When did you cry 'til your heart broke?
Was it a cathartic experience?

When were you forsaken?
How did you find joy?

GAITHER

A Year of Joy: Reflect and Write with Songs and Scripture is a new work,
first published by Dover Publications in 2025.
Illustrations are by Laura Marr.
Line art around QR codes from gettyimages.com
Scripture verses are from the *King James Version Bible*.

ISBN-13: 978-0-486-85536-3
ISBN-10: 0-486-85536-8

Illustrator: Laura Marr
Contributing Author: Stephanie Castillo Samoy

Publisher: Betina Cochran
Associate Editorial Director: John Foster
Managing Editorial Supervisor: Susan Rattiner
Production Editor: Gregory Koutrouby
Cover Designer: Peter Donahue
Creative Manager and Interior Designer: Marie Zaczkiewicz
Production: Pam Weston, Tammi McKenna, Ayse Yilmaz

Printed in China
85536801 2025
www.doverpublications.com